Trauma and the Spirit
Post Traumatic Stress Recovery Guide

by

John Mullaney

authorHOUSE™

1663 LIBERTY DRIVE, SUITE 200
BLOOMINGTON, INDIANA 47403
(800) 839-8640
WWW.AUTHORHOUSE.COM

First published by AuthorHouse 12/12/05

ISBN: 1-4208-2923-8 (sc)

Printed in the United States of America
Bloomington, Indiana

This book is printed on acid-free paper.

Table of Contents

Introduction

This book is based on my true-life experiences going back thirty years. It is only a guide, a rough guide at that. Its purpose is to explore the effects of trauma and what one can do to recover from its aftermath. The chapters are related to events as they occurred. The fourth chapter could be first chapter because the initial stages of trauma started with self-mutilation. The burning of my arms and hands with lighted cigarettes for as long as I could stand the pain. This episode was relativity short lived, thank God, because this emotional pain was most intense. It was then followed by three or four months of anorexia where I lost one-third of my body weight, losing some sixty pounds. I was hardly able to get out of bed without fainting. This also was short lived and passed on without any special effort on my part. Each individual is different and the effects will probably be different for each individual.

There are guideposts within which should be helpful to show a person the way out of the mess which trauma can cause in life. Trauma is what the book is about so it is the first chapter.

The fourth chapter was also important because it was where my first step to recovery began. I had been searching years for help without luck in finding answers to what was wrong with me. There were mental health people, healing preachers, therapists and even a Hindu priest. Finally, it was a kind old priest who was familiar with my condition and understood the situation. Before this meeting I had no idea of what was causing me these problems. We talked a bit and then he prayed over me. It was this that got me on the road to recovery and the dominos started to fall. My case was extreme. This should not be necessary for common problems like depression or panic attacks. Nevertheless, it goes to show how deep these problems can run.

The last chapter may seem a little far fetched but yet it is true. There were no doctors or professional help for me. There were no medications or tranquillizers. It was a journey made through the help of the Spirit and I believe it is a mission mandate of heaven to help the lowly and the afflicted. There is no one more in need of help than someone suffering from PTSD. Scripture from beginning to end constantly tells us that God helps the lowly and to "FEAR NOT". Fear is the main product of trauma.

There is a little bit of esoteric material which might be worth exploring when all the field work is done. By and large it shows conditions which a person could experience in recovering from a traumatic event.

These insights have been obtained through a lifetime of struggling with these problems. They may help a person straighten out his or her life and get rid of a lot of baggage, and maybe get set free.

A book can easily be written on each chapter; however, these books lose the general perspective and overall picture of the nature of trauma. Once an individual gains an understanding of the dynamics, he or she will be able to deal more effectively with the problem. Each person must be willing to do the work and take the steps necessary for recovery. This is a journey. Having an awareness of things to look for and expect while on the path may prove helpful.

The effects and maladies that trauma (abuse) can cause are numerous and devastating to a personality. There was self-mutilation, anorexia, lost of identity in my case. There was also depression, panic attacks and phobias. There were others but these were the main culprits.

There are, however, only two basic underlying features: fear and pain. Fear, because something frightens the person, and mental pain, because of a divided psyche. I had no idea of who I was. The fear limits people's lives. They do not dare to venture out or attempt things because they are paralyzed by the emotion. Beyond every corner there is something to frighten them. The pain drives people into all kinds of addiction: alcohol, drug, eating problems, overwork and even entertainment, anything which will give relief from the mental anguish. In my case I spent the prime years of my life in bars trying to escape the pain.

Numerous personality problems can result because of trauma. They go far beyond the scope of this book. We can, however, deal specifically with several so as to get an idea of how to remedy some of the common problems. Depression, panic attacks and phobias are a few that are born as a result of a damaged soul. The pain of dentist drills and root canals pale when compared to the intense suffering people experience as a result of hopelessness, despair and conflict. These conditions cause pain and torture within the soul. People will kill themselves in order to escape the pain of a divided self.

Depression hurts and it is a tenacious problem. I lost my friends, a very promising future, my self worth and basically my mind. When your hopes and dreams are lost, you begin to see life as a dark scenario. Your soul has been hurt and your mind (part of the soul) will imagine dark thoughts when there's no light to be seen at the end of the tunnel. Not only will depression make life miserable if left untreated suicide can result.

Panic attacks were the most debilitating. They are deep rooted in the psyche. It is a creature born of repressed fears. It is there lurking within the depths of the psyche, ever ready to attack. Terrorized with fear and forced to run for cover, the person is usually too frightened to venture very far from safety. Yet they are surprisingly easy to overcome once you understand what's happening.

A phobia is much like its big brother "panic attack", although not as menacing but always there to ruin your day. The old adage is as true as ever about 'facing the fear'.

There are other problems (psychological) such as compulsions and anxieties, which also result from a damaged soul. Whatever the psychological problems may be, a person wants help and answers to the problem. A remedy for these conditions exists. It requires that you begin to meditate and do some soul searching. This is an integral part to reuniting mind and soul. These problems appear to be mental but actually they require the healing of the soul (psyche). This is where the problem lies and this is where it will be solved.

These problems can be overcome but it takes some effort on the individual's part. Talking to a therapist or a friend helps because this brings the problem into the consciousness where it can be addressed. You can take powerful drugs and sedatives to suppress the nervous system. This may help in the intense stages of pain but this will not cure the problem. To heal the damage done to a psyche requires you to face and overcome these forces within that are creating the condition. This is where it all happens. The soul can restored, and you can expect to lead a much better life. Once you have been healed of the wounds to the soul, you will probably want to go get on with your life. Maybe you might go in search for the deeper meaning in life. Finding the true self, dying to the ego, and ultimately discovering the lost child are all part of the spiritual quest.

It needn't be a long hard road to recovery. When we understand the problem and how to solve it, half the battle is won. The journey has many of the themes of which the classics stories are written. You will have to slay the dragon. Then go between the pillars of doubt. The most difficult is the seeing of one's true self in the mirror. It is not easy but definitely worth the trouble.

Recognition is needed before you embark on any solution. You must know what you are dealing with before a remedy can be applied. Mediation, acceptance and forgiveness are all part of the process of recovery. When your problems are overcome, you will be the better and stronger for the effort. It can be a battle, but it will also be worth it. What is the price for living a normal life without fear and pain? When the wounded soul has been restored, you will then be able to head out in search of those other endeavors. However, until your soul has been healed, it is useless trying to find your true self or your inner child when one lives in a tumultuous sea of conflict. The psyche must be restored to integrity before anything much can begin.

Chapter 1

Trauma

A Hole in the Soul

We live in a traumatic and changing world.

Change causes trauma and trauma is the basis for change. These stresses produced in our society create many psychological problems. The new millennium is coming in fast and furious. As changes occur on earth, one can expect the spirit in mankind to change as well. Mankind is evolving also. An understanding of the nature of trauma is important as it is so prevalent today. Everyone should expect or be prepared to deal with this problem. It is a major factor for so much spiritual disharmony within a soul. Until we recognize what may be wrong and face these problems, we will make no progress in healing the wounded soul. Trying to find our way through life and follow our inner guide when suffering from a damaged soul will only be confusing and frustrating. Trauma and abuse opens the psyche to the dark side of human nature, and until this opening is closed, conflict and pain will affect the individual's psyche. There are many symptoms that can result from traumatic upset. One common effect can be the loss of identity.

Trauma divides a psyche. When dividing the psyche, the mind is also divided. It is one of the symptoms. When the mind is divided, an identity crisis will subsequently take place. A person's perception of himself will change. He may not know who he is now or who he thought he was as a result of the upheaval experienced.

We hear more and more mention of M.P.D. It has been aired on national TV. Sixty Minutes did an episode on the subject. Their feature character was a woman who allegedly had 127 different personalities. It was ludicrous to believe such a story. It seems that M.P.D. is an area which can evoke quite a lot of jokes, indeed, it would seem funny and amusing to anyone who can't understand how something like this could occur. Initially, the idea of an individual having different personalities seems ridiculous. However, below the surface it becomes quite apparent how this anomaly can happen.

This infamy hasn't happened without some substance to the claim. Today there are vast numbers of people who have been emotionally hurt. Broken families, failed marriages, one parent households, etc. Add to this all the stress of the modern world and how fast everything is changing. Is it no wonder that personality disorders occur? People are being emotionally torn asunder. Under these conditions people can lose their moorings and get tossed by these waves of change. They lose the sense of who they are. M.P.D. is the name given to this particular syndrome. It is there as a result of trauma. When you understand the nature of trauma and what happens when you get upset, it is easy to see why this phenomenon occurs. Part of the inherent nature of trauma is to divide, separate or break apart the psyche of a person. It is only one of the numerous problems that can result from a ruptured psyche.

This schism within the mind produces severe mental pain. The pain of a divided self can be unbearable. This pain is probably the worst kind of pain. It is undoubtedly one of the main reasons for the increasing numbers of suicides. People will blow their brains out as a means to escape this pain. With this kind of mental torment one could create a fictitious person as a possible means to escape the problem. Since they cannot bear to live with themselves they produce an imaginary person as a means of coping with their situation. Theoretically one can see how this could be possible. In actuality, however, what most people are experiencing are not M.P.D. but the loss of identity.

When trauma occurs at a young age before the individual gets to properly develop his or her true identity, personality problems will probably set in. It could mean that this person would have been living their life under misconceptions of who they are. They may have been traumatized out of themselves before they got to know the true self. This will extend the healing and recovery process. Since the person never reached that state of maturity, it means they will first have to undo the earlier damage to their psyche before they can hope to find this lost true self.

Your true self will not change but your perceptions of who you think you are can change. A person who has found his true self is able to weather a lot of turmoil and not get upset. However, when a person lives under a misconception of who they think they are and trouble hits home. They can fall to pieces. Their life has been built upon a false self. This can set a person up for a big fall emotionally.

A common remark someone might make who has just been upset may be like this: "I hate what I've become etc. or something like this: "I can't believe this is happening to me . . ." It sounds as though the person is speaking of two different people. Has the person's true self changed or is it merely a different perspective on how he sees himself as a result of trauma. The "I" is merely the ego. It is the false self speaking and has nothing to do with the true self.

Another aspect of trauma is once a person has been upset, then a feeling will be created as a consequence. A simple example of this M.P.D. condition and how a personality can be altered is moodiness. At one time a person seems fine. The next time you meet them they are in an agitated state. It is not pleasant being around such a person. A moody person may or may not be aware that they are exhibiting this trait. A trick the ego plays on us. People familiar with the person will easily pick up on this characteristic. However, the individual who is moody will probably not be aware of it. The person is just not himself. The personality has been altered, only in a small way but it is still quite apparent. The moodiness is produced by feelings and those negative thoughts create this state of being within the person. It is a result of an upset that occurred some time in the past and is being replayed by the mind.

Trauma is the force responsible for all kinds of problems. It is a mechanism that produces a hole in the soul. Also, our fast evolving world produces stress that can also cause a crack in a soul. These forces separate us from our true inner being ... they alter our personality. Phobias, compulsions, conflicts, identity crises are only a few of the resulting problems. Our sense of direction is lost. There can be panic attacks, multiple personalities; and the list can go on and on. Anything, which penetrates a psyche and causes a reaction or change in a person, can create a host of problems. How does one know?

4

A person with a hole in the soul becomes sensitive to various external and internal stimuli; life's energy force cannot be harnessed in a person's center. It pours out like blood into the environment. This energy is the life force of the soul. The hole makes a person open to any and all stimulus as a consequence of this loss of integrity. Situations and people can trigger a reaction in a soul, which, under normal conditions, would not warrant such a response.

Example- A Hole in the Soul

You are walking down the street. All of a sudden, and for no good reason, someone you see causes you to react. You may stop and look at your watch or make some other exaggerated movement like pointing your finger, etc. You do not know why you acted this way. It's like an instantaneous fear attack to the heart. You will be at a loss to understand the reason for this behavior.

When something like this happens, it is a telltale sign of a hole in the soul. Something has or is producing fear in you. Your psyche has been penetrated, and some area of your soul needs healing.

This self-induced internal stimulus which causes a person to react in such a manner is emotion. It is created by some kind of trauma, abuse or fright.

When a person gets upset (traumatized), emotions of fear, resentment, anger and hatred are implanted in the person's soul. These emotions (feelings) are the stimuli influencing the person to react in such a way. It is in a damaged soul that those unwanted dark thoughts and feelings are produced which pour into the mind and affect our behavior.

The behavior may appear to be mental, but the problem is a spiritual one. Those dark thoughts and feelings arise out of a damaged soul. They influence the mind and the way we feel about life. A wounded soul makes these conflicting thoughts and feelings, and they cause much confusion in the mind. A person's discernment is greatly impaired as a result of the conflicting stimuli produced by the wounded soul. The ability to follow your inner guide under these conditions is diminished or rendered inactive as a result of confusion. The psyche is damaged and some healing is needed to restore it.

The damage done to the psyche depends on the degree and severity of the abuse. Simple traumas will cause minor damage to a personality while severe trauma can completely alter or destroy a personality.

Severe Trauma

Going to pieces

All sorts of maladies can be expected. The psyche has been exposed to severe trauma, and like Humpty Dumpty, can end up in a thousand pieces. A few of the more severe problems that can result:

- Depression

- Panic Attacks

- Compulsions

- Personality Disorders

A little girl who was molested by her father will suffer unimaginable pain in her mind as a result of the deep wound to the soul. The forces at work here are greater than ordinary rape, when the father, who should represent trust and a place of refuge for the child, becomes instead a victimizer. There will be a greater violation of the soul's integrity. A deep wound results. This damage to a psyche can be likened to a head-on car crash. Just as the energy of a head-on car crash can devastate a car, so, too, can a personality be affected.

Trauma is a force that separates a person from his or her true self. It alters our personality. We lose our childhood state of spontaneity and joy. That hole in the soul is an open door for foreign invaders. Evil forces can enter and change a person. A person who was a happy, joyful individual can be turned into a mean, vicious creature.

Simple Trauma

An insult, like a poisonous dart, can penetrate a person's psyche and cause a person to begin to harbor feelings of resentment and hatred. Evil has been produced as a result.

Ex. — Somebody screams and shouts at you and you get all upset but say nothing in return. You are burning up inside because of the incident. This alien energy now within you has to be put somewhere or vented. You can take it out on someone else or you can internalize it. Internalizing it means it has to go somewhere. This poisonous energy may end up in the muscles, nervous system or maybe the bones. It will attach itself to something and remain until it is released or broken free. If it accumulates over a long period, it will probably manifest itself physically in some form of disease. The hospitals today are full. Many people are there because of sickness in the soul which manifests itself in some strange physical ailment. Doctors have a difficult time today trying to treat such diseases.

This holding in of resentment will produce bad fruit in a life. A personality will be altered in a negative manner. Even though the insult seems minor compared to the molested girl, there is still damage done. The loss of spontaneity, that childhood characteristic, will result. We begin to hold back feelings because of this resentment now within us. Little children do not hold resentment. Only as we grow out of childhood does resentment (re-feeling) begin to take hold. With resentment, feelings will be repressed and this foul energy is put back somewhere in the body and soul. By blocking and harboring resentment, one will not be able to let go and enjoy life. One will always be living in the past, bound by resentment.

Simple Traumatic Effects

Phobias — Imagined fear with no basis in reality. This is different from a real fear of, say an actual lion attacking you. A phobia is usually associated with some event that caused you to get upset or frightened.

Example — The saying "I was frightened out of my head..." in actuality, the person was frightened out of his or her soul. The soul is now wide open. This evil that frightened you can now enter the person's psyche.

Resentment— (To re-feel). People must become aware of this condition as it is key to a person's spiritual health. Resentment may not seem as damaging as depression or panic but resentment is the main obstacle to letting go and living in love. No small matter when you consider this. A red flag should go up every time you feel that tinge of resentment. It is telling you that something is wrong. Resentment means death to spontaneity and the child within. Resentment means a repression of life's force. All manner of sickness can result from storing this negative energy. A penetration has taken place. An examination of why this happened is necessary to pinpoint the problem. An event, an insult or a matter of some kind wasn't handled properly, you have been poisoned. You must be continually on guard against it. We usually resent or are offended by something of which we are guilty ourselves.

Example — Prideful people don't like prideful people.

Hypersensitivity — "An allergy of the soul"

When a person gets upset they will usually become very sensitive especially to that thing which caused the upset. The person will over-react to stimuli that don't warrant such a response. The stimuli are usually related to the cause of the upset. A person will have feelings (fear-based emotions) produced as a result of some abuse. Hypersensitivity is a consequence of an upset psyche. A person becomes unduly sensitive to certain persons, places, or things. This could actually become a severe problem. A person may not be able to function because of this sensitivity.

8

Example — A Viet Nam vet may be hypersensitive as a result of risking his life for a people and nation that didn't care. He would think about the situation. Why am I risking my life for a people and nation that do not care? This kind of mental conflict can divide the psyche. It can make a person hypersensitive, as the person tries to resolve the issue in the mind.

Some individuals will be more sensitive to events than others. Women by nature are more prone to be upset than men and what may be trauma to one person may not be trauma to another. People with strong minds have a good defense against traumatic penetration. The strong mind being able to focus clearly can keep the soul (emotions) under control. However, all are not so fortunate. Ordinary people when subjected to various crises like the death of their mate, parental abuse, loss of job, cancer, physical assault or whatever, can be traumatized to some degree or another. If one keeps experiencing such events over and over, the more ingrained and deeper will be the problem. A person will also become unduly sensitive in certain areas of life. Also, one can expect that the more trauma experienced will be proportional to the breakdown of a personality.

The little girl, who was molested by her father, will probably be hypersensitive regarding men and authority figures. However, a person can be in a traumatic environment and not be affected. A soldier may be in a life and death struggle, but if he doesn't get upset, then there is no trauma. The events will be like water off a duck's back. When we get upset and begin to react to certain situations, or become afraid for no good reason, that's a sure sign of hostile penetration.

It is trauma that produces emotion. These emotions cloud and darken the mind. Seeing and discerning becomes difficult. One's internal guidance systems go haywire.

The little girl, because of what happened, will view life entirely differently as a result of what has happened to her. Emotions (anger, hatred...) probably have made a home in her through no fault of hers, just as it can happen to anyone who has been traumatized. There are tremendous forces at play, and when opened to these dark forces, they can split a person in two.

Our internal guidance systems will be unreliable until we are healed of our emotions. We will do things we shouldn't do, buy things we shouldn't and go where we shouldn't. Until one can still those forces that cause us to react and control those impulses, a person will probably never be headed in the right direction.

Following the lead of your guide is difficult. It takes fine-tuning to be receptive to one's inner guide. That's why the entire trauma and the feelings produced (anger, fear, hatred, etc.) have to be subdued. You must quiet these raging animals within yourself because it is in the stillness of the spirit that you will find answers and directions. The wounds and holes in the soul must be healed first.

Healing the Wounded Soul

The best guide as to what needs to be done is your own inner guide. However, with trauma you have been damaged in the soul. That's the problem with trauma, it produces feelings. It can be confusing to know what to do. All the feelings that one will be experiencing will have an effect on the mind. These strong feelings which arise following abuse make following your inner guide difficult. However, when you settle down and the spirit is quiet; if you sense in your stomach (gut feeling) that you should do something, then this is what you should do. This is your best guide to recovery. We have all heard this saying, "I had a gut feeling about that." this is the area in the body where your spirit guide guides you. The spirit will not guide you in your mind. However, when one hasn't developed this ability, you can still take active measure to recovery.

Overcoming Trauma

Do — It — Yourself— Recovery

Meditation — "Be still and know that I am God"

It is necessary to first recognize the problem. The enemy must first be found before you can find the solution to your situation. A person who is upset may be unable to cope with the basic demands of life. A person needs time to ponder his condition and find answers. This may sound a little simplistic but many people can be living their lives in depression or delusion and never know it. You must look inward and examine yourself to see what is wrong. This is why mystics and monks go to mountaintops and deserts so they can be alone to find themselves. The ancient Greeks also knew the value in such practice. There is an inscription on a Greek Temple:

Know Thyself

The summation of knowledge

We should not wish to be as the one who is ever learning, yet never attaining knowledge of the truth.

Recognition - Once you become aware of a problem, the light of consciousness must be brought to bear on the fault. This will be painful as no one likes to see faults in himself. It's necessary, however, that you recognize the problem. Until you are aware of trouble and how it is affecting your life and see it for what it is, then there won't be a healing in that area.

Example —*Anger!!!*

When something occurs that really boils your blood and you feel you are on the verge of killing someone, take this time as an excellent opportunity to control that fire of emotion. When a person is able to remain still and not react to the fiery feeling that is blazing within, will be the key to overcoming this emotion. You will feel the heat. It is a real force (energy) but by not reacting and losing one's temper and just observing the rage that is happening with your mind's eye, you will gain control over yourself in this area of your life. Your consciousness will win over your emotion, if you do not react. By watching and passively observing with the mind's eye, you will gain victory over this one emotion. The main objective in soul control is stillness. Do not fight the feeling and the urge to act from impulse, just let it happen and remain still. This same principal applies to all emotions.

Acceptance — You are or have been a victim of some kind of trauma — a dysfunctional family, rape, physical abuse. You must accept that fact ... it is reality. This can be a difficult part of the progress toward healing. Many people never make progress because they see it as too painful. They never make a break-through. Denial is one of the most popular ways of escaping. It can take any form. There's just about no limit on how we can fool and deceive ourselves. All are just different ways of running from the moment. If you continue to deny your situation, you will never be healed. First, you should find someone to whom you can talk. Speaking about the trauma brings it into reality where it can be dealt with, otherwise it will remain in the subconscious to fester and poison your person.

Forgiveness — If you do not forgive, you will not be forgiven. This is a vital spiritual law. It must be obeyed if healing is to occur.

"Father forgive them for they know not what they do."

Chapter 2

Depression is so prevalent today; it's like the common cold. Whenever you get rundown it strikes. It has more than one side but basically it is a spiritual problem, the lost of hope. A person's hopes, dreams and desires disappear, usually in the wake of some traumatic happening. Your ego (the me-thing), just like the little brat that it is, will begin the self-pity parties, and you will be invited. Negative thinking will begin and the mind will be darkened. You will be under the influence of the dark side and unless you can come to recognize what is happening, you might end up dead or spend your life under this influence. If you have ever had depression, you understand.

Depression is an ugly, foul spirit and a robber of life. You have been battered, beaten and have lost all hope and now depression is your constant companion. Life becomes so difficult. A person is hardly capable of doing anything. Going to the store or completing simple tasks becomes a day's work. Washing a few dishes becomes a monumental job. You become paralyzed and there is no joy anymore. Left untreated, depression will become chronic. Then, in time, the idea of suicide enters the mind as a viable option to escape the pain of living.

The problem of depression lies in the fact that your ego (the me-thing) has been hurt. The ego doesn't like it when things don't go its way. Self-pity will be the result. The dark side will want to pull your thoughts down. The dark side works on behalf of your ego. It wants to keep your thoughts in the lower part of the brain; you will never see the light. Seeing the light means death to the self-pitying parties. The lower part of the brain houses the emotions. Self-pity causes the wheels of the mind to spin, producing negative thinking. Negative thinking produces a dark mood. A person needs to become aware of this action. The "I" thoughts will begin and dominate a person's mind. "I" this or "I wish that" or "if that didn't happen to me ..." (ego speaking). This is all the work of the ego. The ego has been hurt and you are feeling it.

Depression is also a spirit, which must be fought and can be fought.

Those self-pity parties can last a long time. The mind attaches itself to those dark thoughts and wants to stay there. However, depression cannot be fought until it is recognized. Recognition has to be made before anything can be done. It is paramount in effectively dealing with the dark mood. A person must recognize the foreboding thoughts, the lousy thinking, as soon as they appear because they will make your present reality a dark one. A person can live in depression for years and never know what it is like to see the light. However, once you poke your head through the clouds of emotion and see the light, you will better understand how those dark thoughts can obscure everything in life.

When you are able to recognize the beginning of dark thoughts and the approaching gloomy feeling, then a major advance will have been made in effectively dealing with depression. You will be able to counter it immediately before you fall too deep into its grip.

Many people live their lives under depression's influence unaware of how it affects them. Until a person becomes consciously aware that something is wrong, no remedy can be applied. Depressions will not only make life debilitating but also there will be confusion and the person will find no resolution to life's problems. As the problem goes untreated, a person may begin to hate himself. The idea of suicide will enter the mind as a way to escape the unbearable mental and desperate situation. The intense pain and conflict can drive a person over the edge. This prompting which can lead one to kill oneself is from the dark side. Trying to escape the pain is understandable. Suicide, however, is a victory for the dark side and the idea must be resisted.

We are all combatants in this cosmic battle. Every single one of us, whether we know it or not, is a soldier in this conflict. Many are carrying badly damaged souls from the ravages of this war.

This conflict within the wounded soul causes a great deal of pain. You can be cursing God one minute and asking God for help the next. If the person can make it through this, it can be purifying to the soul.

"I counsel thee to buy of me gold refined by fire that you mayest become rich." Apocalypse 4:18

That gloomy mood that one experiences with depression is the result of feelings. Feelings are a real energy force. They can drive a person to kill himself. These feelings are your enemy. You must recognize them. This negative energy is stored up in the soul in the form of emotion.

When one "feels depressed" it is because these depressed feelings are influencing the lower part of the brain. This energy, (feelings) that were repressed and not handled properly at the moment when experienced, is now being released. It excites the lower part of the brain and the thoughts produced out of this area do not accurately portray your situation. The mind is clouded in this condition as the troubled soul induced this kind of situation. Everything will look dark.

What you need is a focused mind. This can protect a person from needless pain and suffering. A focused mind can keep the consciousness in the present moment and on the present condition. Example: the dishes need to be done. When your consciousness is focused (your awareness is in the front of the head, area of the third eye), you are able to do the task of washing the dishes even though you may not feel like doing them. The depressed mind, however, with pervading gloominess will have trouble cleaning even a few dishes. Thoughts of how bad your situation is in life will make all things difficult.

The consciousness drifts out of the present moment (third eye area) into the lower part of the brain, the emotional part where you lived your past life's experiences and where unreality resides.

Thoughts of fear, conflict and failure now pervade your thinking. In a short time, you feel like doing nothing. Everything has become difficult because of this shifting of your thoughts. The imagination can run wild like Alice in Wonderland.

The key to solving the problem lies in lifting the consciousness out of the lower part of the brain. This is not easy. Many people live their whole life in the emotional part of the brain. They may never experience a focused mind, a mind that is living only in the present moment. We must remember that God lives only in the present ... not in the past. One s consciousness must be lifted up.

REMEDIES FOR DEPRESSION

1.**Recognition** -- One must recognize when the dark mood is coming. As soon as those negative thoughts start in the head, action must be taken to get the head out of the clouds. This requires a humble spirit. Pride will want you never to admit there is something wrong with you.

2.   **Diet** -- The first step to take when dark thoughts start popping into the head is to eat a nutritious meal. Nutrition is key to remaining out of this area. It cannot be emphasized enough how important nutrition is. Just going without a meal can bring on those dark thoughts. This is especially true for those who have chronic depression. Anytime the body or mind gets bad news or is stressed out, it can fall into depression. Physical exhaustion can be included. Depression has more than one side; it is

also physical. A wholesome diet and lifestyle will go far in defeating the effects of depression.

3. **Lifting the Consciousness** -- Herbs like St. John's Wort are now well known to dispel the gloomy approach of depression. Something must be remembered about herbs. All people taking St. John's Wort will not benefit the same way. To some it may seem to be of no help. If this happens one should try a different herb. Ginkgo Bilboa, etc. may prove move effective in focusing the mind. There are many herbs that work. You must find out what works best for you.

4. **Discipline** — You should engage in some kind of discipline to help focus and strengthen the mind ... for example, the discipline of a college class or the practice of karate. You want to keep the mind, your thoughts, from drifting into the lower regions of the brain. One has to find what works best.

5. **Exercise** — Go for a jog. When the endorphins kick in, the natural high will dispel the depressed feelings. This also releases a lot of stored up energy, energy you probably don't need to save.

6. **Go visit a children's hospital** -- It's amazing how seeing those kids can change a person's perspective immediately. These innocent kids suffering grievous afflictions with such happy faces puts our life sharply in focus when we are feeling sorry for ourselves.

7. **Get a job where you work with the hands** — Working with the hands frees the mind so you can meditate upon other matters.

Anyone of these remedies may be all that is needed to change a person's mood. However, the person must make that initial breakout of depression before the remedies can be used effectively to keep a person out of the depressed state. That ability to recognize how the depressed state affects your personality is important. This determines the effectiveness of the remedies. A person may need to make use of all the remedies in order to stay conscious.

Cure for Depression

A person needs to be born again. This "born again" idea is strange to many people. They don't understand it. It is spoken of in the Bible. "Unless a man be born again of water and spirit he cannot enter the kingdom of heaven." Jn. *3.5*. Religions seldom speak of it yet it is essential to recovery for a wounded soul. Alcoholic's Anonymous speaks of this phenomenon. They call it turning your life over to a higher power.

Your ego and self-will, which probably got you in trouble in the first place, are no longer in charge of your life. A power beyond you takes over. When the person runs out of hope and there's no other place to turn, a person usually seeks and will be receptive to this higher power.

Your spirit guide doesn't want you depressed He finds this offensive. Do not grieve the Spirit.

*The treatment of depression has come a long way in five years. The remedies recommended should be used as a maintenance system. They are not recommended in any way as a substitute for proper medical care.

Chapter 3

Panic Attack

Panic attacks are the culmination of many phobias (fears) and feelings (trauma) that have been repressed. Prolonged exposure to stress and anxiety also contributes to this deep-rooted powerful emotional force. The rapid changes in the world and one's concerns about the future help reinforce these emotions. A lot of damage has probably been done in the soul area. Feelings that should have been felt and expressed are not. For some reason, these feelings (fears) were never felt. Instead, they are repressed, pushed down into the recesses of the psyche. The person is just constantly afraid. This is repressed emotional energy. When unleashed, it is a terrifying force. An individual who has experienced these attacks can attest to that fact. They can make a person miserable, filled with fear and dread.

Panic attacks are phantoms of the imagination. There is no actual reason for the phobia of fear, but the physical reactions in the body are the same as in actual danger. Real fears and panic attacks are similar in that respect.

A Real Fear

You are swimming around in the ocean, having a good time and with no concerns. All of a sudden, the lifeguard frantically blows his whistle and is waving everyone to get out of the water. You look around and see a large fin cutting the water's surface. The adrenaline pours into the blood stream and your heart is pounding. You swim like hell to get out of the water and onto the beach.

A real fear... There was no imagination here. If that shark caught you, you would be in serious physical danger. Note how similar it is to the scene produced by a panic attack.

Panic Attack

You are walking around in a store, doing some shopping, just another ordinary day. Out of nowhere, for no apparent reason, you are seized with an intense fear. Terror overwhelms you ... you have to get out of this place. You're feeling panic, and you head for the door as fast as possible to get away, to get into your car, some place where there's cover.

In both cases, a person would experience the same physical reactions. That flight-fight reaction gives you the power to escape danger or fight for survival if necessary. The intense fear of the panic attack causes adrenaline to pour into the blood stream, increasing heart and blood pressure. There is no danger in reality, yet you react as if there is. You may know there's no reason for this behavior, nonetheless, you are still scared to death when it happens.

The problem can be compounded. When you experience a panic attack, this terrifying force makes you realize that something is wrong inside. For example, you become paranoid and you become tenser. You begin to avoid people, places or things that might cause an attack. You become more self-conscious as you believe that people around you can sense this fear in you. This only makes the problem worse. You really become uptight as you become more afraid of possible situations that can lead to an attack. You never know when an attack will occur, but you know when one happens you will have to make a quick exit.

It doesn't seem to make sense why all of a sudden you become horrified for no apparent reason. There are reasons for this; however, the terror that a person feels is the surge of emotional energy. It comes right up the spinal cord and hits the lower part of the brain. This is where the emotional response takes place. The feelings are real energy but the fear is only a phantom. The energy comes from the repressed feelings that occur as a result of abuse, upset or fright. These feelings have been pushed into the bottom of the psyche. These feelings have to be felt and they will be felt. When someone or something triggers a panic attack, the greater the amount of suppressed feelings, the greater the ferocity of the panic attack. The person experiencing a panic attack can be that child seeking refuge and finds a victimizer instead. A deep wound results. There are deep feelings involved. This damage can be compared to that head-on car crash. Just as a head-on car crash can damage a body, so, too, can abuse disintegrate a personality.

When constantly exposed to these frightening forces, the conscious mind pushes feelings and emotions into the subconscious. These feelings are not handled properly because the person cannot deal with them. Instead they are buried within the body. After some time you become a bundle of nerves and the least stimuli can trigger a full-blown panic attack. Those suppressed feelings of fear will be released. When feelings don't get released, you can expect all manners of physical ailments. This is probably the reason for all kinds of strange illnesses. There's just no telling what kind of sickness can result when a person represses his or her feelings. It is usually fear of some kind that explains why a person cannot express what they think.

Panic attacks must be overcome if you are to enjoy life and if you wish to make any progress along the spiritual path. Living under these conditions is horrible to say the least. It may seem like an impossible situation but these attacks can be conquered and a person can get back to having a life.

How to Beat T-Rex
The Mullaney Maneuver

When an attack occurs and the intense fear strikes, your initial response will be to run for cover. Resist the urge to run. Remaining still in body and mind is the secret. When the panic occurs, remain where you are. Don't run, just stay put, if possible. Remain still and feel the terror rushing up the back and enveloping the head. Don't react, don't move, remain motionless. Remain still and feel the terror of the energy. It's crucial not to attempt to escape by any means. This will defeat the purpose of overcoming the problem. It cannot be skirted in any way. There should be no attempt to make any exaggerated movements, talking out of fear and any impulse to move must be resisted. When you are under a panic attack, this terror of fear will want to make you move in some manner. Do not. Watch with the mind's eye (middle of forehead) for what is happening in your soul, remembering, it is the lower part of the brain that is causing all the commotion. Observe with consciousness the surging terror in your soul but do not react to it. Just watch. It won't take long ... only a few moments. The initial surge of energy will be the worst. Gradually it will wane until it has spent its force. The energy that you feel is the result of all those suppressed feelings coming to the surface. These feelings have to be felt. If handled correctly, this will be a blue-ribbon day in your life.

Each succeeding panic attack will be less powerful and less frightful and easier to control than the previous one. By being still and focusing through the front of the forehead, and not reacting (moving or running away) to all the forces within, you will gain control over yourself. Do not react to those feelings of terror. Just let them flow. By letting them flow, a person will then be finished with them. This is what should have been done in the first place. Resisting them will continue the problem.

What happens by remaining still and watching with your consciousness is like shining a light on the dark force. You begin to see your fears for what they really are, only phantoms with no substance. This focusing through the forehead has to be accomplished for you to appreciate the dynamic difference between the front of the mind and the lower part of the mind.

Phobias

Unreality Has Become Reality

Phobias are another aberrant effect that trauma and life's upsets produce in a psyche. Phobias are an imagined reality and there are numerous phobias. One could develop a phobia on just about anything. There is no reason for the fear that you feel. Yet, nonetheless, you do. It is an imagination of the mind. The person may know this but we are still scared when confronted by our phobias. The urge to flee may be strong, just as it was in the panic attacks. These same physical reactions can be produced, but they are not as powerful. It is really more of a heart problem. Fear attacks the heart ... the center of a person. It can be very controlling.

There are fears and there are phobias. A common phobia is agoraphobia. Some fears may be warranted. It's understandable to be afraid when standing on the edge of a cliff or something like that. It is not natural to be afraid for no reason. There is no apparent danger.

Example – You walk into a hall of people or maybe a Classroom, etc., a small group or even encounter a single person. You become uptight to stop the flow of fearful feelings because you can't seem to handle the situation. This only makes the matter worse. You feel paranoid as you think everyone around can feel the feeling you feel. You may think everyone is observing you. This makes you self-conscious which only exaggerates the problem. You may know there is no reason to be afraid, but you are afraid and you begin to build up blood pressure. Your mind knows that there's no reason for this reaction, but the feelings in the soul have triggered the flight fight system in the body. You feel like an open book that everyone can read.

Phobias inhibit you from enjoying life. Those feelings of fear can keep you from doing anything when there's a chance of being exposed to this situation. This evil can keep you bound up all your life.

Phobias are like emotions. There is some reason for this hole in the soul. Something (a force) has penetrated the psyche. A person has become sensitive (fearful) to certain circumstances, people, or situations, etc. Association with these conditions results in those feelings of fear.

Closing the hole goes as the old adage says: "you must face your fears!" It may look like a scary, snarling creature, and can evoke fear dread. However, it is only a phantom. Repeated exposure to the dread producing stimuli is the remedy ... a little at a time will cure it. When you are in the fearful (phobia) situation, you must stay conscious. Remember what consciousness means? Your awareness must stay in the mind's eye (middle of the forehead) during the frightful condition. If you do this, you will gradually become desensitized to the offending stimuli.

Consciousness means that awareness and thoughts stay in the front of the head. When thoughts drift into the lower part, you will become more susceptible to reacting. Consciousness means not reacting to those feelings that are bombing the lower brain, wanting to get you to react to the situation.

You must let the feelings flow as with panic attacks. Feel the fear but do not resist it the flow by becoming uptight. You will pass through the phobia like a mist. Overcoming a phobia will be a battle, but it must be undertaken and won if you are to gain control of yourself.

Phobias will leave a person at the whim of evil. Little stimuli which otherwise should go unnoticed can keep a person bound up in fear.

Nothing steals the joy of life more than fear. This is a controlling spirit from the dark side. These phobias must be overcome if you are to make progress on the spiritual path. A person suffering from panic attacks and phobias needs repair work for the damage done. This repair work and healing of the wounds requires your overcoming those forces within that are causing you to react to certain stimuli. You become flooded with all kinds of feelings and imaginations from this wound in the soul. When you stop reacting to these feelings, and fears, the hole gradually closes, and you will be healthier and stronger. Your internal guidance system will function better.

Chapter 4

The Devil made me do it

There is another area of the psyche, which can be affected by a wound of the soul. Whereas depression affects the mind and fear attacks the heart, compulsion nullifies one's will. The person's will "to do or not to do" is compromised. He is no longer in control of himself. His will power cannot resist the urging or compelling forces within him. His will becomes subservient to this compelling force. This can produce mental conflict as he does things that he knows are wrong and yet he is unable to stop himself, even when it's to his own detriment. St. Paul understood this inner struggle, "For I do not understand what I do, for it is not what I wish that I do, but what I hate, that I do." Eph. 6.10

You may not wish to do a certain thing, but for some reason, the integrity of your soul has been comprised and the ability to resist is not there. So, a person under the spirit of compulsion has to do whatever that compulsion may be.

Example — Alcoholics, overeaters and other addictions

If you were to ask such a person "why are you doing what you are doing," they would give an explanation that makes perfect sense to them, but wouldn't justify the behavior.

There is a two-fold problem here. Not only is a person compelled by a hostile inner-force, but also the person's ego will defend the behavior. The person cannot admit to this in his conscious mind. Subconsciously, he or she may sense that something is wrong but the ego tells the mind a story which will make everything all right. No matter what the behavior may be and even though it is blatantly obvious to everyone else, the individual's ego will defend the actions.

The ego works in defense of the dark side in human nature. The ego will defend all the actions of the individual, and the person will have trouble seeing the problem in himself.

The mental conflict results when a person is compelled to do something, which he knows he shouldn't do. The mind is influenced by the soul, and the spirit influences the gut. When the soul's integrity has been compromised, the will to resist will be diminished. The ego will win in cases of compulsions until the soul has been restored.

The ego will give justifications to your mind that everything is all right even though in your gut you know that something isn't right. The ego doesn't want the light of consciousness to shine on it. It will always tell the mind that the problem is outside rather than within the person. The ego will prevent you from seeing yourself, as you should. It is an entity unto itself. It has a life all its own and will do everything it can so that a person never comes to see the light, for that light means death to the ego.

A compulsion is an attempt to run away from the light. We run away from ourselves so that the light of conscience won't catch up with consciousness. Eating too much, drinking too much or working too much are all attempts to run away from ourselves. The ego will defend your actions all the way to the grave.

Compulsion can be traced to some soul problem. Anorexia, bulimia and a host of other addictions and compulsive behaviors are the result of a damaged psyche. Life can deal a person a lousy hand of cards. Things can go wrong. We get disappointments and heartaches instead of what we desired and hoped. When these bad things happen to a person, they can experience the void. It is that empty feeling within and the pain that goes with the sense of failure. People attempt to fill the void, anyway possible.

Compulsive eaters — try to fill the void with food

Alcoholics — attempt to escape the present moment by drowning the consciousness in alcohol

Drug addicts — resort to the vast array of narcotics to ease the pain

Sex addicts — try to fill the void with pleasure

Workaholics — work continually in order to keep their minds *off* the issue of facing themselves

These are only some of the more conspicuous means. A person can delude themselves by other ways less apparent. People can use entertainment. By keeping their minds constantly distracted, they can escape the void feeling. A person can be a religious compulsive. They can use religion as a means to hide from themselves. They would also have the moral conviction that goes with it. A person can be praying and praying and praying, yet this can be an emotional reaction, the same as using food or alcohol, just a different kind of attempt to fill the void. It can be the same urge, only this time one uses prayer. It's the responding and reacting to the urge that perpetuates the problem. Smoking cigarettes can easily be used as a substitute to fill the void.

Compulsive eaters are frying to fill this emptiness of the soul and ease the pain with food. Almost everyone has experienced this feeling when something hurts or disappoints us. We head toward the refrigerator to pig out so we won't hurt inside. Filling yourself with food or alcohol, etc. will not cure the problem. Everyone can sense this truth that lies within. It will only get a person into deeper water and can jeopardize his or her life. With the continued use of alcohol and drugs come the addictions. The source of the problem remains and the condition worsens.

Feel the urge; not feed the urge

OOH!! IT HURTS.

Like those other soul problems, meditation and soul searching is needed. One needs to find the exact reason for the behavior. Once again the Art of Stillness is needed to counter the urge to run into a false relief. As a soul problem, feelings are the source of the trouble. The person must learn not to run and fulfill the desire of the urge.

The person needs to feel the urge and not feed the urge. Accept the disappointment and feel the remorse and sorrow of your condition. Acceptance requires humility and when you feel the pain, it will be like repentance. By accepting the pain and feeling the void, the damage in the soul will be minimized. A person should actually move toward the pain rather than away from it. This is contrary to human nature and is thus an obstacle to healing.

A person will begin to grow spiritually when they are able to accept the pain and not run. They will want to cry. This will be like the repentance that Peter experienced. It is not to be confused with confession. "Before the cock crows twice thou wilt have denied me three times." Mark 14.72

By not running a person lets the conscience catch up to his consciousness. The wounds in the soul will heal, and those numerous desires to fill the void will drop away as the soul has no further need for them.

Many people are afraid of this healing process because it hurts. Getting healed from cancer, heart surgery and such illnesses usually requires some degree of pain but this does not stop most from getting well.

BIZARRE BEHAVIOR

Schizophrenia

There is an avenue other than trauma that can cause a penetration of the psyche. For unexplained biological reasons (it's in the genes) a person loses all control of himself; he will be unable to help himself. This is not uncommon today. Mental hospitals are full of such people. They will have behavior that makes them look crazy or insane. They can be hurting their own bodies in some manner.

There is no telling what the person may do. The underlying principal is that the behavior will go against the best interests of the person. These are extreme examples of a compulsive behavior and the person being unable to stop himself. This is not a mental problem but a hostile takeover of one's will. The soul has more than a hole in it. It has a door opened to the dark side. This door has to be closed before any healing can take place within the person.

A therapist may be able to help in other situations and a doctor can prescribe drugs to calm the brain and the nervous system but these will not solve the problem. Meditation, stillness and focusing the mind will not work. When it comes to this kind of problem, a healer of the soul is needed. A person in such a condition needs a member of the clergy or a faith healer.

It is definitely not a do-it-yourself healing situation. You may be able to overcome depression, phobias and other problems yourself. There are things, however, which are not understood. When there's bizarre behavior, you should first seek a religious person familiar with this kind of problem.

A person suffering in this condition may sense something is wrong but will be unable to do anything about it. No matter how bizarre the behavior may be, they will think that this is what he or she should be doing. A person's will has to be put back in command of his or her soul. Numbing the brain is not the way to put Humpty Dumpty back together again.

Self-Mutilation

"... beware of the mutilation." Phil. 3.2

Another area of behavior that is strange and difficult to understand. Why would a person intentionally cut himself with a knife, or why would a person burn herself with a cigarette? What kind of mentality would a person have to do this sort of thing to himself?

Bizarre as it may seem a person gets relief from emotional pain by inflicting physical pain on his or herself.

Emotional Pain = Physical Pain

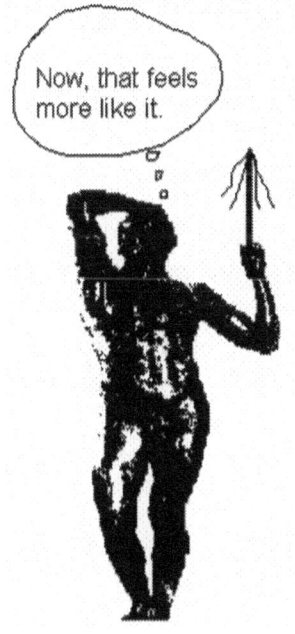

There is probably a self-hatred underlying the behavior and the mode of inflicting the pain is one's personal preference. The pain that the individual is experiencing is the feelings produced from emotional damage. The cause of the emotional damage could come from anything, which upset or hurt a person. An abusive parent, broken family, etc.... The nature of which is probably pretty traumatic to produce these kinds of feelings. The intensity of the pain = the damage done to the soul.

There are probably other things happening within the individual. He could be hearing voices that tell him to cut or burn himself. There will probably be a divided psyche because of unresolved issues stemming from the experience. This divided psyche is probably the root of the torrent of emotion, which occurs within the person. It is a worst case scenario of emotions gone awry.

Hopefully it will only be a short phase to this episode, as it is an area of intense emotional pain. The problem should resolve itself somewhat as a person regains some control over himself. If a person were to continue on this course over an extended period of time, a lot of permanent physical damage could result.

If there were a time to prescribe medication, this would be it. Medication and observation practices are the way to solve most emotional problems. However, with this behavior, there is so much soul damage that the person will not be able to do such things. He needs special treatment. Just as in schizophrenia, it is recommended that a Deliverance or Laying On of Hands be performed. Someone who is gifted with this ability can restore peace to the person and get relief to the person's mind.

Just as Moodiness is akin to M.P.D., Branding and body Piercing is akin to self-mutilation. They are in the same family. It is a common thing today; many teenagers are getting body piercing and branding done to themselves. This is surely one of the consequences of our contemporary society with its broken families, one-parent households and such. These kids are hurting inside. They have a lot of unresolved feelings (emotional pain). They seem compelled to hurt themselves in the name of fad. It is not at the level of self-mutilation but the behavior is related.

Remedy

Christians call it "Deliverance" or "Laying On of Hands." If it works, the will part of the soul is restored to the person. The person will know if some healing has taken place. He or she should feel a sense of peace and feel tired or sleepy if a successful deliverance has occurred.

Chapter 5

"The Kingdom of Heaven is within"

The work done in the previous chapters is needed to restore integrity to one's soul. Those large holes caused by trauma and abuse have to be closed before healing can begin and the true person developed. You should not be seeking the inner child while still suffering from panic attacks, or if you harbor unforgiveness of what your parents did to you. You must also work out solving the problem caused by resentment, for it is the key to obtaining happiness and joy in life. This groundwork has to be accomplished. It's a matter of progression. One event will be followed by another.

You have to dig out of the ground all those old beliefs that have been planted during your life. Weeds of anger and hate, and those deep-rooted beliefs that you used to live your life by, have to come out. The ground has  to be cleared and prepared for the new planting. These are eternal truths and basics, which were taught by Jesus Christ. It's all about healing the soul and getting to know the truth. It's the truth that will set you free. The truth is within one's self. The seeds are there within each person. How a person grows from this seed is a whole different story.

A person's inner guide should lead him in finding what's best. Your inner guide knows what's needed to be done to restore the pieces of the broken personality better than anyone else does. So follow those gut feelings as to what you should do. Once the soul has been healed, it's much easier to follow your inner guide.

Many people are not aware of what's happening within. A strange dichotomy exists after a person goes through a traumatic or stressful experience. The person will resist feelings; especially those associated with the event. He thinks he will not feel. The person becomes hardened. He will not realize that this is exactly where the problem lies. People become de-sensitized to their own person. They detach themselves from what they feel because they do not want to deal with it. This detaching from ourselves causes lack of consciousness.

What we are talking about are those feelings within each of us. Those feelings are the energy in one's life force. The key to getting healed from traumatic experience is being sensitive to this force. Trauma (fear based experience) represses this life force. People may not want to be aware of what's happening within. Blocks to this life force are put up as a defense to these scary feelings. Getting healed in body and soul requires that these blockages and bonds be broken.

Recognition of these feelings is necessary if one is to heal in the soul (raising of consciousness). Until these forces are recognized and acknowledged from within, the person's health in mind and body will remain the same.

The damaging effect of trauma is that feelings (sensitivities) are produced. A situation or experience overwhelmed your psyche and caused a poison to enter you. You may not have handled a matter properly for some reason. Nonetheless, because of this strong emotion of hate, resentment has damaged your personality in some degree. Emotions, not the happy or crying emotions, but hate, fear, anger and resentment are now residing within you. This energy has to be released. When you are continually exposed to this force and it becomes internalized, you won't be able to feel anything after awhile. You become almost impervious to feelings and you gradually become numb to sensation. This is exactly the opposite of what a person would expect. This is paradoxical, yet it is true. It can become a way of life.

Our entire society is becoming traumatized, and we do not know what is happening to us. People become so desensitized that almost anything can happen, and it does not bother anyone. Instead of getting angry at the offending source and returning the energy from where it came, people internalize this poisonous energy in the form of resentment. An emotion (an evil) has been produced. We see this constantly in the world. We are being constantly bombarded with these poisonous darts. They penetrate our psyche and infect us. One can appreciate the words of St. Paul on this matter. He says that "one must put on their armor and carry a shield of faith to quench the fiery darts of the most wicked one." Eph. 6.13. St. Paul was speaking about protecting the soul from attack.

Damage has been done to the soul for whatever reason.

The road to recovery depends on the individual. It doesn't have to be a long process once the person has an understanding of what he needs to do.

The general process of healing from trauma is to quiet the emotions in the soul, which is producing all the trouble. This is done through becoming still. Through meditation you become aware of what's causing the wheels to spin.

In meditation, you acquire the ability to be still. Stillness is where you want to be. This is why meditation is important. Being alone is needed. It is in stillness where you will find the answers. In modern times, being still is almost impossible. Our way of living means rushing here and rushing there. This makes it difficult, but being alone is essential. Meditation leads a person to recognize the problem within, and then the acceptance and forgiveness are needed to restore the soul. These steps need to be taken in order to progress.

Meditation

The Art of Stillness

Meditation is a process of recovering and healing the damaged soul. Through meditation one finds the problems within that motivate behavior. "One finds the beam in one's eyes." People never see the beam because they never look inward.

Meditation shows a person that something is wrong. You become aware of what needs to be corrected on the inside. You begin to see the damage done by trauma, and how your personality is affected.

The problem encountered trying to meditate is that the ego will try and stop this from happening. It is entirely against the ego's interests. The ego doesn't want you seeing yourself and what's wrong. Pride and ego will work hand in hand to distract you from meditation. They will fight the light of consciousness from exposing the dark nature within. They will defend themselves. Pride never wants a person to look at himself as being wrong. The ego will always justify' the actions of pride. The problem is always outside of the self. The other person is always at fault. Pride and ego keep a person in darkness. The light of consciousness means death to them. They will tell the mind any and all the reasons that are necessary to keep a person from recognizing that the source of the problem is in them. The ego's best defense is its camouflage. It does not want to be seen. It works undercover away from the light of consciousness. It opposes the true self.

One must not get meditation and praying confused. Praying is important and God knows this world needs a lot of it. However, people can use praying and religion as a substitute for meditation. Praying can be used as alcohol or drugs or music can be used. It can be an escape to keep the mind off one's real self. Religion can be used as an opiate. People can get all filled up with religion and their feelings and use this as a distraction. Religion will remove attention from themselves. Not one correction or failure of the soul will be achieved, but they will sure feel good about themselves. You must be careful not to be carried away.

Meditation shows a person where the problem lies. There will be a pain as the ego and pride is exposed to light. It is here when most people run away. They cannot bear the pain. People numb themselves with all manners of means to cover and not feel the pain ... alcohol, distractions, praying ... anything, which helps them escape. They should, instead, move toward the pain, feel it and observe it. A person has to feel the pain that consciousness has brought to light through meditation.

With the awareness of the fault now present in the mind brought there through meditation. Consciousness and stillness is needed while this light burns the infection away. One has consciously accepted the fault and now bears it to the light consciousness. In a brief period of time, one has been healed of the problem.

Acceptance

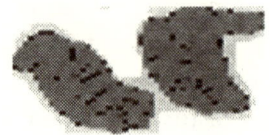

One has become aware of a problem through meditating and has come to recognize and accept the situation. Until these steps are taken, the problem remains hidden. This may seem pretty obvious at first glance. However, one who has been victimized may not be aware that there is a problem that needs to be addressed.

Ex. — Low self-esteem. When one realizes that because of being a victim of a traumatic experience, his opinion of himself has fallen below his capabilities, "okay," he says to himself, "I have low self-esteem. How do I get rid of the problem?"

The consciousness has been made aware of the problem, which is important. Victimized people many times will not see clearly because emotion clouds their minds. However, once recognized and accepted, remedies can be applied, then you can begin to build upon your talents, which everyone is endowed with from birth. Finding these talents is part of the rebuilding process that will restore integrity to the damaged soul.

Forgiveness- A Spiritual Law

You have to forgive the person who victimized you. If there is hatred or resentment toward your victimizer, then your wound will never heal completely. There are spiritual laws just as there are laws of physics. Resentment and hatred must be given up. Resentment and lack of forgiveness are like poison in a soul. Jesus continually taught this. Love your enemies, not because you are a coward, but because of the danger which harboring hate does to the soul. Resentment in a soul destroys life. You cannot advance spiritually as long as resentment remains within your soul. Resentment will hold a soul dead in its grip.

Chapter 6

PEELING THE ONION

Let me out of Here!

Life's traumas and problems and hurts combine to produce layer upon layer of false beliefs, misconceptions, and false personalities. The real you lies at the core beneath all this false information on which you base your life.

To peel the onion requires work to find the real you. The real you lies buried under all those layers. In order to protect itself, that little child that was once you, had to build these protective layers. It began to get hurt as it grew, and this defensive mechanism grew in response to these abuses. How many layers there are depends on the individual and how much he or she has been through in life. These layers have to be stripped off to free that inner child.

There are guideposts that can help in this backtracking through life. With these markers or guideposts, one may or may not initially realize that he has passed from one area into the next. In other words a layer of the onion has been peeled. One must develop this sensitivity to spiritual matters. However, when still on the path it shouldn't take long to realize that a boundary has recently been crossed. It is somewhat like traveling through one state into another. It may take awhile before you notice the change in features. One shouldn't expect to immediately move from the Plains State into the Rocky Mountain State. It will probably be more of a gradual change of scenery. The process of peeling the onion is a matter of going back in time and re-experiencing the various stages of life. By re-experiencing them we will be free of them and will then be able to pass through on our journey back in time. There may be areas that are frightful and unpleasant, but it all must be re-experienced.

The first layer is pride. This is a difficult first step, not because it is hard. It is because of the illusive nature of pride. This is the protective shell of the ego. Pride will keep a person totally blind about himself. He never gets to first base and starts the inward journey because pride will have him look elsewhere. Pride would have him go in search of glory, honors and money — all things that are outside of the inner man and which help to reinforce the ego. Pride will not stand for any introspection, as it will have the person believe the problem lies outside of himself and that he is always right no matter how sick the person is.

This first layer, pride, is the outer shell to the inner man. To break this shell, a person has to catch himself or herself in the **Action of Pride**.

Example- someone has just done you a favor. It may be small or seem inconsequential. For some reason, however, you didn't thank the person. If you did it was forced and not a genuine thanks. Something within held you back.

When this happens, the person needs to examine his or her motives for acting this way. "Why didn't I thank that person? He did me a favor." They need to meditate on the situation.

Why dost thou see the speckle in thy brothers eye and yet dost not consider the beam in thy own eye. Luke6:42

A person needs to be constantly aware of this motivating force in his or her behavior. When a person senses this' Action of Pride', a little humility is needed. Pride is a very curious thing. Those who have the least reason for pride tend to exhibit the most pride. It's the same process for spiritual as well as materialistic pride. Pride likes to keep you in the dark when it comes to learning about yourself. Pride will keep a person totally blind about himself. He never gets to first base and never starts the inward journey because pride will have him look elsewhere. Pride is primordial. Pride is spiritual. It was the first sin, the sin of Lucifer.

There is no remedy for the prideful man.

Pride

This shell of pride has to be broken before any work can begin in removing the layers of deception that lie beneath the surface.

Pride can come in different forms. There can be intellectual pride, spiritual, materialistic, just about anything which leads one to believe more highly of himself then he should.

Intellectual — You think you know everything. Those degrees and the letters after your name can easily lead one to think very highly of himself. It's the stuff that makes for a hard shell of pride. It won't be easy coming out of the lofty nest. It is a trap that the ego can set. A person locked in this shell could never come to see their faults. Knowledge of self is true knowledge. Today, we are ever learning but never obtaining true knowledge.

Spiritual-

People can make themselves believe they are saints because pride will tell a person, "You are so good! You pray and give alms. Don't worry about the way you mistreated that person." As long as they don't look inward, pride keeps itself intact. There is no rocking of the boat and everything remains the same.

People can get all puffed up with religion, believing that going to church makes them so good. They can't be doing anything wrong. This also is a trap set up by pride. One may have all manners of faults and be oblivious to them.

Materialistic-

This is very common problem in the United States. Material things seem to be the only concern for people. Not much value is placed on spiritual gain. People's only focus in life is the seeking of money. They give little or no regard to the inner person. Pride would have it as such. Until a person comes to this recognition he will not get the entire picture. Pride is a set of blinders. It forces an individual to look away from himself.

Once the blinders of pride have been taken off, you will begin to see things in an entirely different perspective. This is especially true for people recovering from a traumatic experience. There will probably be a lot of emotion that needs to be looked at and controlled. Once pride has been broken, the individual can develop his true potential. You will see that it's the blind leading the blind out in the world.

False Beliefs

People grow believing what society, church and even our parents, God love them, have told us. Even though they probably mean well, all those beliefs and values of the church, state and parents are their own values. Their values have been laid upon us and the vast majority of the time they are accepted as truth.

The real truth is knowledge of ourselves. This is the truth that will set us free. This truth lies within each person. When we die, the church, the state and our parents will not be responsible for our lives. We go into the next world by ourselves and are ultimately responsible for the truth.

Let us not deceive ourselves. People go to church on Sunday because of a belief system. Their spirit is wrong when they go because they feel compelled to go. They should go because they want to go. Religion creates these beliefs and people, without a thought, naturally submit to the pressure. These pressures can cause conflicts within a person trying to find himself and align himself with his religious beliefs.

Example – Catholics can have a lot of internal conflict trying to resolve the issue of sexual behavior. Baptists have a problem about drinking alcohol. Yet, Jesus came eating and drinking. The Amish can have a conflict over using electricity.

When a person follows the higher power within, his life is not bound up in doctrine. This is not recommending a free license but a discipline in response to one's inner calling.

The teachings of our parents will have to be examined also. One can almost certainly expect that his parents have passed some misconceptions of life onto their offspring. Mankind has been doing this since Adam and Eve. The cycle has never been broken. Occasionally, there is a soul that breaks the mold, but as a rule, the same beliefs pass continually on and on. You may have had wonderful parents; however, this shouldn't make their views on life the same views you unquestioningly accept. Each individual is unique. This uniqueness makes everyone different.

All those beliefs and values of church and state, and even your dear parents may not necessarily be yours. People carry around a lot of baggage because the society in which we live lays this weight on us. People expect everyone to be, more or less, like themselves and behave the way they think they should behave. This conventional stuff will have to be discarded, if one is to progress toward one's true self.

As you progress along the spiritual path, you can expect to have corresponding changes in your physical being. Your eating habits may change for the better. Lifestyles will probably change. The body will begin to heal itself of diseases. It will become stronger and more youthful. There is a direct link between the spiritual healing and physical healing.

Ego Death

A giant step spiritually. It's incredible, yet probably true that the vast majority of people have no idea of how their egos operate. The ego is a tremendous driving force in a life. Ego, however, is a monster. A two-headed monster ... the other head is pride. Until pride is broken, a person will not be able to deal with ego because he will not be able to see it. Ego cannot bear the light. The ego does whatever it wishes.

Groups like Alcoholics Anonymous know about this monster. It is an entity unto itself. They call ego death by a different phrase. They call it "a releasing of self to a higher power." It usually happens when a person hits rock bottom. Their ego is usually responsible for getting them there. You hit rock bottom when there's nothing more left in you to carry on the way that brought you where you are now, in a real mess probably. Christians call ego death as "being slain in the spirit." Ego dying will feel just like you died. Something, indeed, has died your ego. Your ego power has been exhausted and there's nothing left. That self-driving force is gone. It is all your false identities that the dark side instills about you in your mind. The ego will not want to give up this power. It usually has to be forced into surrendering, as it will fight to stay alive to save its nature. The upside to ego death is that the individual now relies on the universal power of God's love to govern his life. Christians call it being "born again."

A soul that breaks the shell of pride and has experienced the death of the ego has come a long way. That person will know the value of spiritual things. The world will not honor this but the person will know himself, in his heart, of its value.

True Self

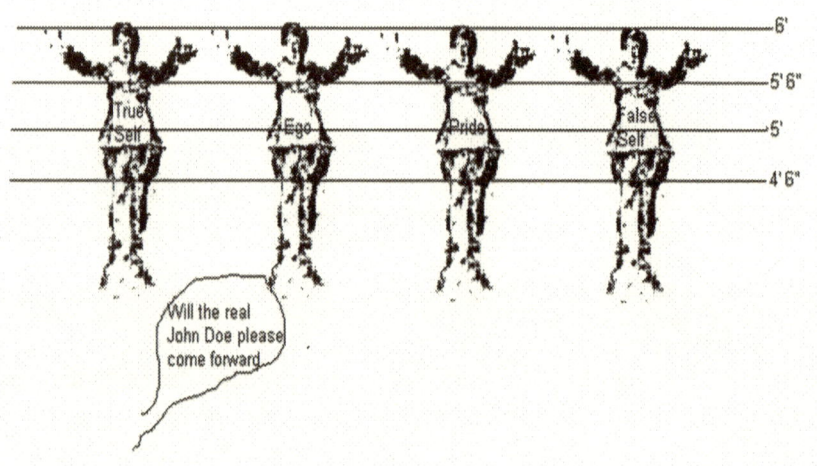

Getting to know the true self requires removing the false layers. When a person removes a layer and exposes more of his true nature, his consciousness starts to be more in tune with the universe. When layers are removed, he also sees his fallen nature more clearly. This is the area where few dare to thread. In an ancient story when the boy sees his true nature in the glass, he runs away and cries. Mystics allude to this part of the journey as seeing oneself in the mirror.

There's a peculiar thing about seeing our true self. Other people see our true self better than we can. It is very much like pride in this respect. For some reason, we cannot see or have difficulty in seeing different attributes in ourselves, yet others see them so plainly. It is only by breaking pride, removing the junk, and experiencing ego death that a person can begin to see some of his true nature. One's true nature comes through when a person loses consciousness of himself or herself. It's when the mind is totally focused on something outside of itself. This secret of losing oneself is much sought after in the areas of sports and acting. Various disciplines such as of traditional karate tries to develop this essential characteristic of a person.

Example — When you played the best you ever played. It could be in any field. Maybe playing the best game of basketball you ever played. You may remember the game but during the game you cannot remember yourself. You lost consciousness of yourself along with what you were doing. This loss of self-consciousness is being in a different zone. These moments of being in this zone are probably experienced by us all. It is when we play beyond ourselves. The higher power is now being engaged. Staying in and living in the zone is what is difficult.

INNER CHILD

"Unless you become as little children, you shall not enter the Kingdom of Heaven."

The Kingdom of Heaven is within, and all the previous work you did is to get here. Those layers have been peeled off. The previous groundwork has restored the soul's integrity. One now tries to unleash the inner child.

That little child has been pushed down into the background by life's experiences growing up. It wants to come out and play. There are obstacles, however, holding it back. The first is fear. The inner child may not consider it safe to come out. No matter what we do, fear can always turn up and ruin things.

There's another emotion more sinister than fear. It is resentment. This will certainly block the free flow of life's force. Resentment, when harbored within a soul, will always block the opportunity, and joy cannot be achieved. That releasing, a freedom found by the complete abandonment to the flow of energy, would not take place when a person resents something.

Resentment destroys the free flow of energy and dampens spontaneity. There could be a lot of reasons for the resentment. It could be jealousy, envy or hate. It could be anyone of these and more.

You should meditate on the problem and find out what is holding you back. You must find the problem that's causing the resentment and get rid of the emotion.

Releasing the inner child and living life as a child is the ideal objective. It takes full commitment. There is no holding back from the flow. Anything, which is destructive to an individual enjoying life and living life as God intended, must be avoided. Instead, work on releasing the inner child. Releasing the inner child requires faith. One must have trust and confidence that it will be safe to come out and play. Living life as a child is where love triumphs over fear. Love and trust are major characteristics of a child. Perfect love casts out fear.

As individuals trace their lives backwards, they should expect to re-experience certain times during their lives... adolescence and young adulthood. This regression is needed to reach that into that area of innocence.

Example -- A middle-aged man trying to go backward to find that lost child. You come to that area of your life when you were a fighting young buck. How do you go through something like that again? You know you can't go around beating people up. When you're forty something you just can't be doing stuff like that. However, you must pass through this stage of life if you wish to proceed on your journey.

When you get that pugnacious spirit like you felt when you were young, you must not try and deny it ... it has to be faced. You must not fear it because it is only a phantom. If you must get pugnacious, then it must be done. You cannot duck the situation because of the consequences. This is only the work of the phantom. There may be similar times in your life. Maybe not the same, but the principal will remain the same. These phantoms are obstacles blocking your spiritual progress.

You want to become like the child you were when you were young. It's a journey of backtracking one's life. By backtracking and re-living, re-experiencing the areas of your life, you are able to clean the slate and purge away all the trauma and garbage that has accumulated during life. You walk backwards and feel the pain of any trauma, if necessary. The pain may be what someone did to you. You must feel and forgive. If you do not forgive, the progress will stop there. The more you can go backwards, the greater will be your spiritual advance. This journey will be a natural progression, once you get on the right path.

Chapter 7

Mind Control

So you have closed all the holes in the soul and the wounds are healed. However, the mind still hasn't been controlled. Negative thinking can cause a lot of trouble in a person's life. For example, you can get fired from work. Suppose you were thinking lousy stuff about your job which, in turn, creates a bad attitude. This produces a negative energy field, which your boss picked up on. Personal relationships are lost or never started because your bad thoughts poison the air. Thoughts are real entities. They have an energy all their own. If you think negative thoughts about anyone or any situation, people will pick up this vibration energy. Maybe not consciously, but in their gut they feel it.

Thought control will be especially important after one's soul integrity is restored. The life energy that once poured out of the holes is now being contained in the person. This gives more force and energy to a body in all capacities. A person's thoughts have much more energy now, and this can be used in a positive way or a negative way. Be careful of your thoughts.

When you have succeeded in plugging the holes and overcoming the obstacles, you will be stronger. This strength of spirit must now be controlled in the mind, another part of the soul realm. The soul's energy is now focused in the brain as the emotions have been overcome. This new found energy could cause a lot of trouble for the individual when his thoughts are not right.

There are naturally gifted people with strong minds just as there are naturally gifted people with strong bodies. A strong mind provides a wall of defense against emotional thought produced from upsets. However, this is not the general case. Most people will have to work on conditioning the mind to keep it in focus. Emotional upheaval will cause the consciousness to drift into the lower brain. It is here where the negative thinking occurs or maybe the mind will drift like Alice in Wonderland. The mind, when not focused, can come under the influence of emotion.

The mind is part of the soul. Like the soul, the mind will need to be healed. This will naturally come of its own when the other work has been done and one is on the right path. "Be renewed in the spirit of your mind and put on the new man." Eph. 4.23. You will be able to control thoughts that were uncontrollable before. A person will be able to stop the negative thoughts and thinking, which they were not able to do before. In Christian terms, they call it "Renewing of the mind." It takes time and patience, but it is part of the healing process.

You will be able to see things more clearly, both your own situation and others. You will be able to keep your mind off yourself (egocentricity) and you will be able to monitor your emotions, and keep them in check. It is the culmination of the repair work of the soul.

"Awake, sleeper, and arise from among the dead, and Christ will enlighten you." Eph. 5.15

Enlightenment is similar to the Renewing of the mind in that they are both products of the mind resulting from spiritual growth. Enlightenment is a discovery that happens when a person is able to raise his or her awareness out of the lower self, that pre-programmed, emotionally based, follow the crowd mentality. When a person grows out of this lower area of the mind, they will recognize how they were programmed to live a certain way because of the influence of parents, church and state.

The Eastern religions write much on this idea of enlightenment. The Western religions never mention the idea. Each religion professes it has the tenet for reaching an elevated state of spirituality. Each religion offers their path as the best way to the top. Yet most of the roads look very similar. The Hindu path to the mountaintop isn't much different than the Christian path. Ultimately, they all lead to the same destination. They all merge at the top where self-knowledge is found, not ritual.

From this view the true self can now see all those hindrances which made the trip difficult. They can see clearly the obstacles and pressures, which were exerted, on them during the ascent.

The person can look back and see how they were not their own person. People can be programmed just like animals. The media: television, radio and the newspaper can easily influence and condition people's minds. Pavlov was a scientist who conditioned dogs. When Pavlov rang bells the dogs would immediately react by salivating. Custom, culture and the opinion of others likewise condition people. When people read, hear, or see something, which the media produces for its reactionary effect, people respond as predictably as a trained or conditioned animal. We do not move from our center of intuition and knowing, but are led by these external influences.

People move as though they are blind. This is because we have no self-knowledge. Remembering what the ancient Greeks said, "Knowing oneself is the summation of knowledge."

This programming is quite evident. Society today promotes not only the loss of individuality but also the loss of sexual identity. This merging is not of natural design but from other powers. There is no longer male and female but the unisex culture. Society is also promoting the integration of races. People grow up believing these beliefs to be truth. It is not questioned but accepted as though this is the way it's supposed to be. Society can condition people's minds into believing what they want them to believe.

This conditioning makes it easy to control people for political and other purposes. In medieval Europe, the religious were the educated people at that time and the church had the power and the influence over the lives of the people.

An enlightened person should be able to recognize this programming and see the influence that it exerts on governing lives and beliefs.

Enlightenment is not only the ability to recognize external but also internal influences. The emotional state of mind will prevent a person from thinking clearly because the consciousness will not be where it should be (center of the forehead).

When a person gets upset there will be a shifting of awareness or consciousness in the mind. A person susceptible to this influence must be aware of it. A simple example of this shifting of awareness:

Try to figure out some math, computer or other problem, which requires some mental thought when you are upset. You will understand this state of awareness when you see how difficult it is to focus your mind and figure out the solution when you are in this state of mind.

This is just a temporary upset. In a little while, after you calm down, you will probably have no trouble solving the problem. People can spend their whole life in an emotional state of mind. An angry person, for example, would be constantly reacting and this would cause a shift of consciousness. A person who experiences trauma at a young age may live in this state of mind and never be aware of their condition. The more emotional a person is, the less they will live in the present moment. Schizophrenics, for example, live in a world far removed from the reality of the present. As a person grows and matures inwardly, they will become more aware of this higher state of mind where everything is clearer.

Some people, like the Irish, are inclined toward the emotional state whereas the Germans operate mainly from the logic side of the brain.

People who operate more out of the right side of the brain will be more susceptible to this shift of consciousness than the left-minded person. Women, thought more intelligent than the male, when upset, can become quite illogical. The woman, having access to more sensory information, will also be more sensitive emotionally.

The left-brained person will have the stronger, sharper mind. Logic and reason will govern them. They will not be influenced by feelings. This is a difficult area for the sensitive person who operates mostly out of the right side of the brain. This is where the discipline of the mind becomes important. It requires that a person keep his or her mind on what they are supposed to do and do it even though he or she doesn't feel like doing it. A person should be able to recognize this influence of feelings on the mind. Unless a person is aware of this influence, he or she may be living a life in an illogical, unproductive manner. They will never think clearly because they are being influenced by feelings.

Being left-minded doesn't mean a person is enlightened. A person may have the awareness of a wild animal or the education of a Ph.D., yet know nothing of this state of enlightenment. Enlightenment results from the spiritual journey. The ability to govern the desires is part of this endeavor. The desires for money, sex, power and fame are given the back seat to the development of the spirit.

Enlightenment is an experience. Words can only speak of it. A person becomes more enlightened when he gains more knowledge of self. With the increased knowledge of self, a person becomes aware of his or her shortcomings. This awareness is part of the enlightenment process. A person will manage to see the "beams" in their own eyes and pay less attention to the "speckle" in other's people's eyes. It results from the quest to conquer one's self. It is a spiritual awakening, which may or may not be religious in nature.

Enlightenment is not the end of the journey but the beginning of a new one. You are no longer governed by external and internal influences. One is led by the higher power. You are not a slave. You will have been "set free." You can recognize programming and handle your emotions. You will no longer be driven by the herd instinct. You are your own person.

It seems illogical but as the world changes, people will be living more and more in their right minds.

Another area of consideration concerns the Mary-Martha Syndrome. This occurs when a person's thoughts are continually in one world. They can be either in this world or the other. Depending on whether one is in the Mary condition or the Martha condition.

As the story goes; Martha was busy doing all the housework while her sister, Mary, sat at the feet of Our Lord. Martha complained to Our Lord about it. Our Lord replied, "Martha, Martha, thou art anxious and troubled about many things, and yet only one thing is needed. Mary has chosen the best part, and it will not be taken from her."

What was Mary doing? She was meditating. As Jesus said, "My Kingdom is not of this world." This is all well and good, but a Mary condition can also lead to trouble. If a person stays in this world, they may have no idea of the reality of the other world; the one in which they are now present and must exist.

It would seem, however, that the vast majority is not affected with the Mary condition but rather this world suffers from the Martha condition.

Aura Imprinting

The New Age Philosophy speaks of things such as the Aura*, vortexes, crystals and many other esoteric topics. These things do exist. However, they will not make any difference on the spirit walk. They will not help but only feed the mind with pride.

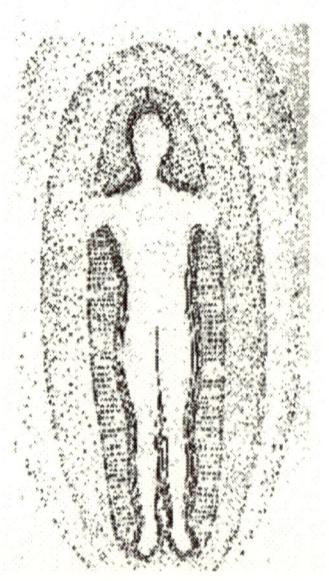

A person is not sensitive to these energies until they are sensitive to what is happening within themselves. This only makes sense. How can one distinguish these external influences yet unaware of what is happening within their own universe?

Ordinary people may be subjected to these influences and never know it. Negative and positive energy fields are quite common. Some are small, such as a room or single building while others could encompass a large region.

People will be affected with this energy in either a positive or negative way depending on the polarity. An evolved individual with a more develop Aura will be susceptible to Aura Imprinting. The Aura is the energy field surrounding all living things. It can be imprinted by the energies of their surrounding environment and vice versa. This energy whatever it may be will residue in the Aura and can be picked up by other people on the subconscious level. If a person is sensitive in the spirit then their Aura should be able to carry an Imprinting.

Example:

Spend an active evening in some energetic atmosphere. The energy from the environment and people will be picked and carried in the Aura. The next day when you come into contact with people they should sense this energy in your Aura and make some kind of reference to it. It will be on the subconscious level. They will sense it in the spirit but will not be able to understand why they made reference to it.

Leshya- (Sanskrit: "light, "tint"), according to Jainism, a religion of India, the special aura of the soul that can be described in terms of color, scent, touch, and taste and indicates the stage of spiritual progress reached by the creature, whether human, animal, demon, or divine. The leshya is determined by the adherence of karmic matter to the soul, resulting from both good and bad actions. This adherence is compared to the way in which particles of dust adhere to a body smeared with oil.

*"leshya" Britannica Online

The jiva, or soul, is classified according to the good or bad emotions that hold sway. Thus the saleshi ("having leshya") are all those who are swayed by any of the emotions, and the aleshi are those liberated beings(siddas) who no longer experience any feelings, neither pain nor pleasure, not even humor. The three bad emotions (ill will, envy, and untruthfulness) give the leshya a bitter taste, harsh or dull color, a smell that can be likened to the odor of a dead cow, and a texture rougher than the blade of a saw. The three good emotions (good will, union with goodness, and nondistinction) lend the aura the fragrance of sweet flowers, the softness of butter, a taste sweeter than fruit or honey, and a pleasing hue ranging from bright red to pure white.

If your soul spirit is not Aura Imprintable, then you need to develop more in the spirit. Rubbing two crystals together does not do this. The New Age speaks all about this kind of stuff. However, one cannot achieve these abilities by their means. The New Age Philosophy encourages the development of the ego. It teaches the empowerment of the self. This is exactly the opposite of what is needed. Spirituality is dying to the self. The onion has to be peeled.

Points to Ponder

Nutrition plays an important part in brain chemistry. When a person feels tired, food can stop undesirable thoughts from being produced.

What is in your mind produces corresponding energies to be produced in the psyche, which are transmitted out of your being into the surrounding area affecting people and things either positively or negatively (Aura). The extent of this influence depends upon the depth of feeling within the person.

When the consciousness is unaware of one's self, the true self emerges. Keeping the consciousness watching over the emotions in the soul and not reacting, just watching, is key to control of self.

Chapter 8

Dream Therapy

"He dreamed that a ladder was set up on the ground with its top reaching to heaven: angels of God were ascending and descending it." Genesis 28:12

When a person gets upset, feelings are initiated. During the day these feelings can play havoc with our internal guidance system. It will be frustrating to follow our guardian angel, inner being ... whatever you wish to call this guiding force. Discernment becomes difficult. A person can be lost and confused as to what to do. However, you still have another guidance system that is available to you. Dreams!!!

When one experiences trauma, emotion will inevitably result as a consequence of the upheaval. You may not know where you stand during this time. Your sense of direction may be off, and the guidance from your inner spirit will be distorted. You may not know which way to turn. This is a time when you should try to get in touch with what your dreams are trying to tell you. Even though it looks like nonsense, your dreams are trying to help you find the way back to health and happiness.

When a person gets upset during the day, it would be common and expected to have dreams during the night as all those feelings bubble up into the subconscious mind in an array of thoughts and images. This may be dismissed if due to an occasional upset or whatever. However, if a person has been traumatized, he or she will continually have dreams as the subconscious tries to sort through all the upheaval within the person and get the psyche back into a state of composure and harmony.

During the night, those feelings will also flood the brain. With practice, however, you will be able to understand what the subconscious is trying to tell you. The subconscious is far better equipped to deal with the various array of problems than your present conscious mind is able to. Solutions to your present condition are available when you are able to tune into your dreams. To tune into your dreams, a person should make a conscious effort to instruct the mind to remember the dreams before going to bed. This conscious effort seems to reinforce the subconscious to be alert and ready for the dreams when they appear.

A person must be receptive to his subconscious. His dreams will show him things he needs to see and understand in order that he may get well.

He will probably see things, which he is afraid of and may need courage to face. This should be expected when one has been traumatized. Trauma will produce fear. However, his dreams will show him what he needs to do and the person's spiritual advancement will depend on the person's response to these matters.

With trauma a person can be expected to have an identity problem. He may have no idea of who he is. M.P.D. will probably be evident. Maybe a person is just immature and hasn't developed into an individual. Under such conditions a person's dreams will first have to reveal to the person his or her identity and where they are in the universe. This will take time and patience to develop the rapport necessary with one's dreams. It's a matter of progression. Little by little will the pieces of the psyche be put together. In time a person will have the vivid dream which they know is the real thing.

Some people will be more inclined to dreaming than others. People who use the right side of their brain more in life will probably dream more than those who use the left side. This same principal applies to those who are more receptive to upset. Those who use the left side are probably the more focused and logical in the affairs of life. They seem to be less susceptible to traumatic upset. Those who use the right side will be more receptive to intuitions, hunches and the leadership of the spirit. Accordingly, they will be more sensitive to emotional disturbances and easier to upset.

Initially, a dream dictionary will help in understanding what some of the bizarre images and events could mean to you. Also taking a class on the study of dreams would help you to become more familiar with this unseen world. After awhile you should begin to know intuitively what your dreams are saying to you

It will take a little time to develop the ability to interpret your dreams. This can depend on several factors. If a person has suffered a lot of damage like Humpty Dumpty, one should expect a longer initiation time. With trauma, a person may have an identity crisis and have no idea of his or her true identity. It will take time for the subconscious to sort through the disorganized psyche and get connected with the conscious. Like a computer, it will go through all the thoughts, feelings and emotions and display them for you to see. It may be difficult at first to tune in for guidance, but the answers will be there. It's just a matter of figuring out what the meanings are. As a person becomes more centered, the understanding of dreams becomes easier and more focused.

Your dreaming state will go hand-in-hand with your spiritual condition. When you are an emotional mess after trauma, your dream state will reflect this accordingly. Also, some people are more receptive to the dream state. The right-minded person will be more responsive to this state than the left minded person.

The person who is more developed spiritually and in tune with their dream state should not have much trouble figuring out what his or her dreams are saying, even after a recent upset or trauma. A minor upset or whatever should not set them back too much. This would not be the same scenario as the person who hasn't developed his nature. Since he is not sure of his identity, it will probably take longer to develop the ability and confidence to trust in the dream state. Like Humpty Dumpty, who fell and was broken into a thousand pieces, it just takes longer when there are more pieces to be put together.

You should be aware of certain precautions. Eating too much or drinking too much can induce dreams. Dreams under these conditions shouldn't be considered seriously. This also applies on those days when there was a lot of upheaval. You can expect that emotional energy will rise up during the night, and produce a lot of chatter in the dream state. However, when one is in a troubled condition, either through abuse or trauma, dream therapy offers a great deal of information to you which otherwise you would never know.

You will find that as you begin to heal from the damage done to the soul, nightmares will drop off. Dreams will be easier to follow and interpret, and they will also become less frequent. As you begin to get control of your emotions, there will be a corresponding response to your dream state. As the confusion in the soul subsides, so also will be the confusion in your dreams. Dreams will be easier and clearer to understand as you make progress arising from your fallen condition.

An example of the growing influence of dreams in life is the Craig Rabinowitz story. The prominent Philadelphia lawyer was leading a double life. He ended up strangling his lovely wife and leaving an eighteen-month-old baby girl. Initially, Craig Rabinowitz denied the charges even though the evidence was there for everyone to see. It seemed like it was going to be a repeat of the O.J. Simpson story.

Everyone was shocked and surprised on the opening day of the trial when Craig Rabinowitz admitted to the murder. The front-page headlines of the city paper reported the story.

Rabinowitz Admits to Killing Wife

A dream urged him to "do the right thing"

Thus ended one of the most sensational
murder cases in this region's recent history.

Philadelphia Inquirer

October31, 1997

Craig Rabinowitz goes on to tell of the influence that dreams had on his decision. He speaks of his condition at the time of the murder, six months earlier.

"I lost my ability to know right from wrong.
Right became wrong and wrong became right.
I believe that my mind just was not able
to know what the right thing to do was."

This example of how dreams affected a life isn't an isolated case. It seems to be a growing phenomenon. Caution has to be maintained if one is going to live according to what the subconscious reveals. That individual has to be somewhat self-actualized. The person has to be healed from soul damage and has grown in the spirit. They have left behind them all the baggage of conventionality, religion and social stampings. Following your dreams will help a person get there. However, investing your life savings and starting a new life or career are serious decisions. They can greatly affect a person's life. The person must know for certain that they are self-actualized and can trust their dreams.

The subconscious can be a friend and guide who will help in solving life's problems. It can be the key to revealing a person's true identity and the source of help to many difficulties. Dreams are a way of accessing this vast array of knowledge. Dreams can show future events and can shed meaning and light on situations that are puzzling. They are always there to guide a person through the difficult as well as the easy times.

The adage "Let me sleep on it" is more relevant today than ever.

Chapter 9

Following the spirit

"To do or not to do," that is the question. We are all familiar with those feelings that tell us to do something or go somewhere. "I should have done this"; "I knew that was wrong"; "I had a gut feeling about that." All day long, in every life, this same scenario takes place. The $64 thousand question is "How do we tell the difference between these two eternal voices?" Different groups of people seem to possess an uncanny ability to listen to that inner voice. Successful people seem to have this innate sense, often described as "women's intuition." This may defy logic, yet how often is it correct? Little children instinctively know the difference between good and evil. Most people, however, never fully develop this ability because something knocked them off course during their life. There are numerous obstacles that can keep a person from following his inner guide, some of which have been mentioned. There are also certain prerequisites that should be met before a person can get back on track and develop confidence in this course of direction.

PREREQUISITES

Healed — A person cannot follow the inner guide (guardian angel, gut feelings, etc.) under the influence of uncontrolled emotions: anger, hate, and fear. These emotions need to be overcome as they cause too many disturbances within a person as to distinguish between the sources: the soul or the spirit.

Ego Death One cannot follow another lead when one's ego wants to do something else. A person's ego will be contrary to the inner guide. You cannot have both worlds. Alcoholic's Anonymous calls this: giving up of sovereignty of one's life to a higher power. Religions have different names for it. Christians call it "being born again." You must make the commitment if you are to advance spiritually.

Desire -- "If we live by the Spirit, by the Spirit let us also walk." Gal. *5.25.* To follow your inner guide, you might expect to do a lot of things you ordinarily wouldn't do. Not only must you dispense with your ego and the way you would do something, but also you must undertake tasks that require motivation. To build a relationship with your inner guide will require interaction. It is not a one way street. The spirit may lead you to face the demons and dragons that lie within you. Unless you have a strong desire, you will run away at this point.

Fast — Not necessary but beneficial in helping to distinguish between the feelings of one's own desires and your inner spirit.

Following the inner guide requires surrendering of one's will. One's will and mind must be receptive to the prompting of the inner guide. It also requires faith as it is like being led while wearing a blindfold. The relationship takes time to develop, and all the groundwork in the preceding chapters has to be done, otherwise one may end up following one's own desire and not the inner guide. "Do not believe every spirit but test the spirits to see whether they are of God." Jn. 4.1. The inner guide operates through a person's spirit, not their feelings. Sometimes it's very difficult to tell them apart. A sensitivity to that still small voice which bids us to or not to do must be experienced to be fully developed.

Example — The phone rings. You receive a check in your spirit. (It's that tiny hesitant feeling in the gut region). Your mind and conditioning tell you to answer the phone. The check said "no." You answer the phone and in an instant, it is confirmed in your spirit that you shouldn't have answered the phone.

Example — You go to the supermarket. The number of items to choose from is enormous. You are in the frozen food section. You really don't like fish but you get that prompting to open the freezer door. You get a confirmation in your spirit about a certain box. It doesn't make sense to you but you take it home, and when you go to eat it, you find there are three frozen filets in a box that said only two should be there.

They are only small matters but all day long over a period of time a relationship is established. A building of trust takes place. Your spirit guide will instruct you and lead you in all things.

Example — You feel hungry and are thinking about eating something, however you sense the prompting of the Spirit not to eat. The forgoing of your meal is an act of faith. It required that your desire was subservient to that of the spirit's lead. It also required that the mind had to be disconnected. If there was questioning and looking for explanation, the matter would be a lost opportunity. A short time later you received an invitation to dinner from a friend. Through such minor things a rapport with your inner guide is developed.

When following your spirit there are certain guideposts, which will help in understanding the way.

Knowing the Ropes

Expect to be tested — it is a matter of faith and you have to be 100% committed. We can only fool ourselves. Your spirit guide knows your situation better than you do. The spirit is not confined to only certain areas of living. All matters of one's life must be committed to the spirit's leading.

Belief Systems - what a person has learned to believe as true may not necessarily be the truth as the spirit sees it. All the beliefs and values of parents, church and state are not necessarily the values of the spirit. The quicker you get rid of your beliefs, the sooner you will be able to follow your spirit's lead. You cannot develop mind-sets as this may prove an obstacle to where or how the spirit can lead. You must keep an open mind. All those beliefs and values may be limiting as the spirit will not be able to instruct you and develop you in the way it needs to.

Example — You owe money to someone. You are going to the mailbox to mail the check. You get a check in your spirit. Your spirit tells you not to mail the check. Your reasoning tells you to mail it or you'll be in trouble; it can be a serious matter. A week later, something more urgent happens, and you need the money.

The reason you got that check was your spirit guide trying to tell you something for your own good. The issue of right and wrong would have caused you to mail the check because it seems to be the right thing to do. However, these beliefs of right and wrong in one's mind have to go. When one follows the inner guide, it's a matter of faith and not reasoning. Your spirit guide wants to help you. Operating from your own ideas of what to do, based on your own reasoning, will not work.

"Put your thoughts aside when you follow the inner guide."

The ability to follow your inner guide will result as you do work on the inside. It's all a matter of getting in touch with our inner selves and the Kingdom of Heaven that is inside each of us. This is also where you will find the truth, which will set you free. Your spirit guide will lead you to do what is best for you. It will probably be not what you had in mind or what you desire. The priority of the spirit guide will first be the integrity of one's soul, not making money or sex, etc. "Seek you first the kingdom of heaven."

To follow these higher powers requires the surrender of one's will. Your will is the only thing that belongs to you. It is the only thing that God wants from you. The spirit guide will not and cannot override a person's free will. This is a working relationship like a horse and a rider ... you being the horse with blinders on it, the spirit being the rider. The spirit can lead if you permit, or you can kick up your heels and say no.

How to Tell You Are on Track

1. Timing —"arrival on the dime"

The spirit may lead you around the block or on what may seem like a wild goose chase. If, however, you show up at a certain place at just the right time, then you know you were correctly following the lead of your spirit guide. There was some reason for the delay, maybe in order for you to run into someone or just a small test of faith.

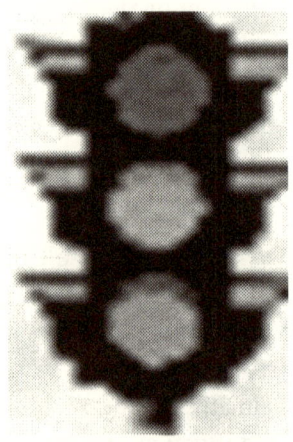

2. Positive signals

You are not sure but you sense the leading of the spirit so you step out and follow the lead. Somebody or something confirms this feeling by a friendly greeting or possibly a set of green lights to where you sense you should go. Maybe someone opens a door for you. It may only be a small matter, but it's a sign you are on the right path. It is only a baby step but it's developing a sensitivity to the prompting of the spirit that is important.

3. **Confirmation**

You are stepping out in faith, believing you are following the spirit's lead, but not positive. Someone will actually confirm that what you are doing is correct. They will probably not be aware of this but confirmation is a sure sign to you that you are on the right path.

4. **Signs**

You sense the spirit guide is telling you to do something and you are dead-set against doing it. You start kicking up your heels. You look for a sign because you don't believe.

Example -- You sense the spirit is leading you into a place you really don't want to go, a bar, etc. You ask for a sign. Your spirit tells you to put a coin into the poker machine. You do and you win some money. It confirms that you are where you are supposed to be.

There must be some reason for the spirit wanting you in there at that time. Sometimes, you may not know if you are being led by the spirit guide or by just your own feelings and imaginations. One good clue is that when you feel like doing something because it would please you, then that's a good indicator that it's your own desire and not the spirit's prompting.

This is why the emotions have to be controlled. Distinguishing between the prompting of the spirit and the prompting of the soul can be difficult and confusing. Fear, anger and a hurting soul may be doing the prompting. Those reins that are guiding you may not be of the spirit. Also, the work of de-programming your beliefs will now come into play. If you hang onto all those old beliefs, you will never be able to follow the inner guide, as this will create problems. "Do not pour new wine into old skins," scripture tells us.

It takes times and patience to develop sensitivity to your inner guide's leading. Those checks you will get in your spirit are your inner guide trying to tell you something. However, as in any relationship, problems can cause strains, cracks and a possible break-up. A person's will and desires will inevitably clash with those of the spirit guide. Mistrust and disharmony can develop and can be expected. How long the break-up lasts depends. It could be like a one-night stand or the relationship could turn into a real love affair. How deep the relationship develops depends on this interaction. No matter, your spirit guide will always be there if there is a spark left.

Problems Encountered

Trying to follow the inner spirit's lead can be confusing, especially when you start out. To build a foundation, all the previous groundwork has to be done. The emotions have to be under control. There's no use to even bother to follow the spirit's lead until you become conscious of what's going on within yourself. Otherwise, you will just end up banging your head against the wall or pulling your hair out. You will quit before ever getting started.

There are numerous problems that can throw a searching soul off track, or cause one to follow a wrong lead.

Getting Upset -- The wheels of the brain will begin to spin, one's thoughts and imaginations will run wild. Under this condition, all kinds of stimuli are active in the mind, and you could easily fly off in the wrong direction.

"Be still and know that I am God"

Fear -- The main weapon of the enemy to keep a person bound. When you are full of phobias and fears, the evil one can play with you like a cat plays with a mouse. If you get a prompting to do something, and fear attacks, you should try to proceed, as the first prompting is from the good spirit. You should be careful when following a prompting under *fear.* Your own frightened soul could be producing the impulses to do something. It could easily be the motivating source. Mistaken beliefs can predominate when the soul isn't calm.

Confusion — When you don't know which way to turn, pride and ego will probably be the cause. Humility is essential. When humility is lost and you set out on your own power, you are open to attack by the spirit of confusion. You are no longer under the guidance of the true guide. The break will leave a person aimlessly drifting. Every road will be a dead end or a false lead. No fruit will come of it.

Questioning??? — I think, therefore, I don't know which way to go. You are led through your spirit. Once you begin to use your head and start questioning this and that, you will lose that connection in the spirit and the lead will be lost. It's a faith thing, and reasoning is contrary to spirit walking.

Disobeying -- The moment you disobey your inner guide, a second deceiving spirit will immediately take over, and you will begin aimlessly going around, and nothing will come of what you are now doing. No positive result will occur. You should just call it quits and wait for the next inner guide's prompting.

Example — Your guide leads you down a road for some reason unknown to you. You begin to question and reason about what's happening. The spirit guide cannot override your will. This action of questioning on your part will drive away the true spirit guide. A succeeding spirit guide will take over. It will be a false and misleading guide. Whatever you do will come to naught. You did not like the idea and naturally rebelled against it. This questioning will cause a problem. You will lose the lead when you do this. This same problem will occur the moment you disobey what you know you should be doing.

The leads of your spirit guide and the leads of second false spirit will be similar. You may be able to sense this loss of true guidance, but you may not sense it. The only way to tell the difference will be in the fruit produced.

Following your inner guide can be a way of life. The ability is available to everyone. However, with the modern world and its fast paced way of living, it is seldom realized. This is a dynamic and working partnership. It's developed over time, and trust is the binding element. It is constantly in flux, and a person must be 100% receptive to successfully follow the spirit's lead. A person must remember that the spirit guide is your guardian angel. It wants to help you get well. It's there to do what's best for you. It is the priceless pearl. As we approach the millennium, we can expect changes in the spiritual world corresponding to the changes in the physical world. Those who are receptive to the spirit will be transformed into new people

Behold I make all things new.
Apocalypse
21.5

www.trauma-n-spirit.com
Mullaney_john_t@hotmail.com

www.ingramcontent.com/pod-product-compliance
Lightning Source LLC
Chambersburg PA
CBHW030402290526
45785CB00004B/1877